TITIAN

ABOUT THE AUTHOR

Denys Sutton is editor of *Apollo* and art critic to the *Financial Times*. He has contributed to most of the leading art journals. His publications include studies on Bonnard, Derain, Staël, Toulouse-Lautrec and Whistler. He has just completed a revaluation of Rodin.

FOR CASPAR

DENYS SUTTON

Titian

BARNES & NOBLE, INC.

NEW YORK

Publishers • Booksellers • Since 1873

Editor: Anthony Bosman
Lay-out: Wim van Stek and Aart Verhoeven
Published in the United States in 1963
by Barnes & Noble, Inc., 105 Fifth Avenue, New York 3, N.Y.
© 1963 and printed in Holland by The Ysel Press Ltd, Deventer

Titian is a painter for lovers, for all those, like Swann in Marcel Proust's "A la recherche du temps perdu", who delight in the beauty of the female body . Yet although a master of erotic suggestion, he was also a man who felt, and felt deeply, the call of religious faith; sensuality and credence were not incompatible in his personality. He is likewise a painter for those captivated by the direct appeal of paint as such (not that he worked *alla prima*) and his actual handling of pigment and his intricate way of building up a composition reveal much about the refinements of painting.

The customary image of a picture by Titian is probably of some magnificent beauty, a courtesan with ample bosom and abundant hair, the fitting companion to a Venetian sensualist, or else the portrait of an elegant patrician. This image is certainly correct but it requires to be complemented by another one — that supplied by one of those late canvases in which the essence of a grave episode from the Christian story, the anguish of loneliness perhaps, is rendered by means of sombre yet enticing colours. One must make no mistake: although Titian was never an intense expressionist like Tintoretto he used a rich palette and introduced structural novelty into his composition.

Titian's art has not unduly suffered from the buffets of fashion. His range was so considerable and his style so varied that his painting is able to please different tastes. The grand evocative manner of the last phase, when he became so radical and impressionistic, did not altogether accord with the ideals of artistic excellence cherished in the 17th and 18th centuries. Yet our generation has especially appreciated just this final outpouring of his genius—those canvases in which his bold experiments with colours resulted in an ever more sonorous and even musical chromatism, and in which much was staked on pictorial freedom. Indeed, he was perhaps the first artist consistently to emphasise the qualities of pigment as a substance; his colours thus form independent and inherently exciting areas which correspond to, and express, the mood of a composition. This conception is central to his pictorial practice. No insuperable difference, therefore, intervenes between Titian and the modern spectator. His art is eminently accessible; and in the eyes of our irreverent and impatient age, he does not rate as a stuffy old master, lacking relevance or meaning. On the contrary, the distinction of his craftsmanship (about which Charles Ricketts wrote so perceptively) heightens the interest in his painting. An indication of this capacity to arouse contemporary curiosity is surely reflected in the controversy provoked by the cleaning of certain of his pictures in the National Gallery, London: the argument has waged fiercely because Titian retains his hold over young painters and critics.

Titian's exact date of birth is not known: the limits, as given in the written sources, are from 1472 to 1482 or later. In any event, he attained an immense age as he died in 1576 and, what is remarkable, remained in the forefront to the very end. He was a natural master of the avant garde, whose essential flexibility of character and acute sense of survival allowed him to forge ahead.

He was a true conservative, well aware that imprisonment in a doctrinaire approach could prove fatal and that a pragmatic evolution was essential. The long span of his life coincided with a period of turmoils and changes, amongst them Venice's war with the League of Cambrai; this forced him to leave the city in search of fresh employment. But his ability to face up to trouble was remarkable; so was his sheer exuberance, the vitality which prompted his attack upon so many different aspects of painting. There was no weakening in his endeavour: only, at times, a siphoning off of wearisome tasks to assistants. He himself ever remained at the helm, inventive and ready to accept the challenge of new commissions.

Titian's art is intoxicating. He was so positive, so determined, so set on giving his own personal interpretation of a theme or a sitter. He did not flinch from the sort of treatment which could have stirred up trouble with his patrons. Any 16th century artist who had to work for imperious men, as was so often the case, had to keep an eye cocked on their demands and to observe the winds of change, or, at any rate, in which direction they were blowing at any one moment. Titian, who was exceedingly crafty, learnt how to manoeuvre his fellow men. From his close friend Aretino, that audacious "scourge of Princes", he picked up the art of conciliating his masters; in the end, Titian, one feels, more or less had the whip hand.

Titian was an impressive personality, with a definite hint of steel in his make-up. The "Self-portrait" (p. 9) at Berlin could as well represent a financier as a painter; the left hand, depicted almost as a claw, is so powerful and even grasping. The late "Self-portrait" (p. 77) in the Prado at Madrid is equally revealing. He portrays himself as a true Prince of Painting; venerable, noble and resigned; but a sharp old gentleman still. In the dangerous days in which he lived, Titian was anxious to be on the safe side; for one thing, he prudently invested part of his profits in land. He carefully cultivated his relations with the Serenissima at Venice, with the Estes, the Gonzagas, the Roveres and with the Spanish court. Thus he was in the position to secure the measure of independence and security essential for the creation of his art. One significant result of his achievements was to raise the artist's status. He was no journeyman painter who did as he was told; far from it; he was a rather independent person quite prepared to keep potentates waiting for the fruits of his genius. He endowed art with an importance, in international terms, which it had not really possessed until then. "What rich man would not have liked to have his portrait painted by Titian?" declared Sansovino in his account of the splendours of Venice, published in 1581. Cannily, Titian had taken advantage of this situation and of the increased secularisation of art.

Titian's career is a success story. He was a youth from the Venetian hinterland, from Cadore in the mountains, who made good in the great city. He was the artist who was to fulfil innumerable important commissions; who was to paint the now lost "Battle of Cadore" for the great hall of the Ducal Palace at Venice; who was to venture to depict a Farnese Pope, as in the picture at Naples (p. 52), with something of a caricaturist's verve; and who was to become Court Painter to Charles V, a Count Palatine and a Knight of the Golden Spur. His success and his example opened the way for similar aristocrats of art—Rubens, Van Dyck, Velázquez and Delacroix; and their debt to him was in terms of status as well as in terms of inspiration.

He arrived in Venice, between 1496 and 1499, at an auspicious moment. Venetian painting was in the midst of a full and generous development; there was no dearth of talent to vie with, and from which nourishment could be derived; no lack of splendid examples on which to found an approach. Any painter of energy and imagination would have been heartened by what he came across in Venice. According to his early biographer Dolce, Titian first studied under the Zuccati, who were mosaicists, and who presumably did little more than train him. He then entered the studio of Gentile Bellini, later passing into that of his younger brother Giovanni. The Belli-

Self-portrait
About 1550; oil on canvas; 38×29½ in.;
Gemäldegalerie, Berlin-Dahlem

nesque ingredient in Titian's formation was by no means negligible. Giovanni's poetical style and his warm colours surely enriched the young artist's palette, and evidence (derived from Vasari) indicates that the pupil assisted the master, notably in the famous "Feast of the Gods" in the National Gallery, Washington. (Later in the 1520s Titian revised the picture, adding a landscape background.) Moreover, a link with Giovanni is suggested by some of his early religious pictures.

Nevertheless, his real point of departure was Giorgione. It seems fairly certain that Titian worked with him in 1508 on the decoration of the façade of the Fondaco dei Tedeschi (now destroyed) and their connection was so close that a collaboration between them must be envisaged. Pictures like the "Concert" in the Pitti Palace, Florence, and the "Concert Champêtre" in the Louvre, might almost have been executed with the express purpose of teasing experts! Giorgione's attraction for Titian was understandable. How could any sensitive spirit—and he was certainly that—resist the poetical lyricism of Giorgione's art? "Giorgionismo" is fundamental to an understanding of the early Titian. Yet within the artistic language which Giorgione formulated and which Titian adopted, the differences between the two men are as boldly writ as their similarities.

To say this, of course, is to criticise neither artist nor is it to take sides; it is simply to maintain that their fundamental preoccupations, the passions which motivated them, were really dissimilar. Giorgione's art was narcissistic and withdrawn; it was concerned with symbolism of an intellectual nature; it was a form of confession too. But Titian, even at his most Giorgionesque moments, was always direct and down to earth; his poetical sense, which should not be underestimated, was tempered and directed by an enthusiasm for the tangible.

Thus in an early Bellinesque picture like "The Gipsy Madonna" (p. 19) at Vienna, he brought out the femininity of the Virgin. Like all, or nearly all, his female sitters she is a beautiful woman and uncomplicated; by no means the mysterious creature who appears in Giorgione's "The Tempest" in the Accademia, Venice. Only towards the close of his life did the undertone of melancholy, which tinged Giorgione's art, manifest itself in Titian's. The contrast between the two temperaments, in fact, was very real; it is neatly illustrated in the "Concert Champêtre" in the Louvre, in which the hands of both artists may be discerned. The woman on the left is by Titian for the excellent reason that she possesses the radiance and modelled fleshiness so typical of him; and these qualities are absent in her more wistful companions. However, it was Giorgione's example, his radical extension of the painter's scope, which helped Titian to concentrate on the feasibility of celebrating pleasure in his work. And circumstances, namely Giorgione's death in 1510, allowed him to take over the succession.

The young Titian had a vivid appreciation of all that was well rounded and lovely. The series of beautiful women, dating from the 1510s, of which the two most splendid are the "Flora" (p. 25) in the Uffizi and the "Salome" (p. 23) in the Doria Gallery, Rome, have immense appeal. It was typical of Titian's response that, despite her gruesome task, Salome's expression is tender. How coquettish, too, is the strand of hair which caresses her cheek! Quite early, he also revealed a grasp of human psychology. This is shown in "The Tribute Money" (p. 22) of about 1518 in Dresden, painted for Alfonso d'Este, Duke of Ferrara. And the individual character of the protagonists is so aptly rendered that we are left in no doubt that this is a testing moment: a moment of truth.

In the 1510s, Titian began to show his mettle. His lucid way of placing figures in space and his sense of harmonious relationships are stressed in the "St. Mark with Saints Sebastian, Roch, Cosmas and Damian" in Santa Maria della Salute at Venice, painted in about 1511. He was intellectually alert as well. One instance of his receptivity to other men and of his concern with artistic procedures, in the formative years when he was close to Bellini and Giorgione, was his appreciation of the significance of Dürer, who had been in Venice in 1494-5 and 1506-7. His debt to the Northern master is possibly confirmed by the early "Madonna with the Cherries" (p. 27) in the Kunsthistorisches Museum, Vienna. Besides his work as a painter, Titian also executed a remarkable series of woodcuts, the "Triumph of Fate" (about 1511); these indicate that his aim was not so much the production of attractive small pieces, but, as Tietze once remarked, of designs which could vie with frescoes; in short, a form of public art. But in them, as the same authority remarked, "all Giorgionesque modernity has been abandoned in favour of Mantegnesque solemnity".

Titian's individuality and compass are revealed in the three frescoes in the Scuola del Santo at Padua which, if not the earliest of his works to have survived, are the earliest to which a firm date—they were finished by December, 1511—may be assigned. They are sometimes apt to be rather underrated in any account of Titian's development; yet they are highly fascinating; that representing "St. Anthony Healing a Newborn Child" contains a Roman sculpture in the background as well as a cut of landscape. The frescoes show that he could take the sort of narrative manner associated with Bellini or Carpaccio and give it a modern twist. "The Jealous Husband" (p. 24), for which a pen and ink study exists (Ecole des Beaux-Arts, Paris; p. 13) treats of a clash between individuals, a subject which intrigued him in later years.

In another respect, Titian revealed his hand. This was in his growing passion for landscape. In Venice, the mid-15th century

The Jealous Husband
About 1510; pen drawing; 7⅜×6¾ in.;
Ecole des Beaux-Arts, Paris

painters Carpaccio and Giovanni Bellini had already appreciated the marvellous potentialities of nature and in the latter's "Stigmatisation of St. Francis" in the Frick collection, New York, the saint is almost dwarfed by his surroundings. For the Venetians, nature provided plenty and repose; warm-hued hills, streaked skies, and brownish grey rocks acted as the appropriate setting for pictures, both sacred and profane.

Giorgione's conception of landscape was an idealist one, which drew its sap from his local surroundings. And he stands behind Titian's early landscapes. The differences between their viewpoints are obvious enough: Titian's rendering is essentially that of a masculine painter. The debt to Giorgione is acknowledged in the backgrounds of the "Baptism of Christ" in the Vatican Gallery, Rome, or in the "Noli Me Tangere" (p. 26) in the National Gallery, London, with which his colleague's name has been associated; these are individual all the same; these, in fact, are paintings by a man to whom the trees, fields and seasons were very real—and this is also shown in his rare drawings. In his paintings, he delighted in shafts of light which pick out the colouristic content, especially the bold blues. They may lack Giorgione's tender sweetness but their vitality is a compensation.

Equally imbued with "Giorgionismo" is the landscape in the two famous poetical pictures—the "Three Ages of Man" (p. 28) in the Ellesmere collection (now on loan to the National Gallery of Scotland) and the "Sacred and Profane Love" (p. 29) in the Borghese Gallery, Rome. Titian is an idyllic painter in these two pictures—in the manner of a poet from the Greek Anthology; direct, free, pleasure-loving. Inevitably much critical ink has been spilled on interpreting the exact meaning of "Sacred and Profane Love", but its mood has been best characterised by Sir Kenneth Clark. He wrote in *The Nude* that "to anyone who looks at Titian's picture as a poem and not as a puzzle, her significance is clear enough. Beyond almost any figure in art she has what Blake called 'the lineaments of gratified desire'."

A beautiful passage in this picture is the sculptured relief, visible on the sarcophagus. As antique sculpture appears in what seems to be one of his earliest pictures, the "Pope Alexander VI and the Bishop of Pesaro before St. Peter" in the Antwerp Museum, one may conclude that, almost from the start, antiquity meant much to him. It was a constant interest and, as Vasari noted, his visit to Rome permitted him to enlarge his knowledge of its virtues. Yet Titian was not a neo-classicist in the strict sense of the word nor did he litter his pictures with fragments disposed for their picturesque effect. Antiquity was a source which replenished him; thus many are the figures, at different phases of his career, which seem to hark back to some classical stature or relief. The almost honey-coloured figures on the sarcophagus—a wonderful passage of illusionistic painting—are imbued with that controlled movement typical of 5th and 4th century Greek sculpture. It is as if Titian could dart back into the past and perceive the qualities of Greek sculpture even through the Roman copies which mainly came his way. Titian's dependence upon the antique still demands closer examination and his familiarity with Greek originals may have been more extensive than is generally supposed; it is just possible that he had the chance of seeing the collection of antiquities formed by Cardinal Domenico Grimani (died 1523) and his nephew Giovanni Grimani (died 1593); these contained various fine works of high quality and the majority are now in the Museo Archeologico at Venice.

Both this picture and "Three Ages of Man" are static compositions—they present a moment of arrested time. Such is their intention. However, this note of repose was to be abandoned in "The Feast of Venus" (p. 34) in the Prado, the "Bacchanal" ("The Andrians") (p. 30) in the same Gallery and the "Bacchus and Ariadne" (p. 31) in the National Gallery, London. All three were painted in the 1520s as decorations for the *camerino* of Alfonso, Duke of Este, at Ferrara and are characteristic examples of the humanist interests of the day. The libretto, which was probably supplied by the Duke, is derived, in the first two works, from descriptions of imaginary pictures given by Philostratus, a late classical writer, and in the third, mainly from Ovid's *Ars Amatoria*.

The rhythm of the dance in the "Bacchanal" and the general movement in the "Bacchus and Ariadne" may impose a sort of unity on the pictures; but they are not composed by means of a continuous interlocking process; they are made up of sections. In fact, all three works can be divided into splendid details (pictures within a picture) and their full visual meaning occurs once these have been digested and seen in relation to the whole. In the "Feast of Venus", the statue of the goddess is a presiding genius; standing aloof she forms one segment, while the landscape, with the roof of the house glimpsed through the trees, is another. Movement is derived from the women who dash into the picture space from the right; their alertness gives point to the vivacity of the children, whose individual personalities are so charmingly rendered.

The way in which the children are arranged, streaming into the middle distance, would suggest that Titian was not unmindful of the problems of perspective. This was not one of his main concerns but he could play with such effects brilliantly, as is proved by the "Annunciation" at Treviso.

Titian's admiration for antique sculpture presumably led him to distribute the figures in the "Bacchanal" as if on a frieze. For all their number, they fulfil their role; they are like a corps de ballet. But the picture is not hieratic; Titian prized the significant gesture and used it to vary the movement in a composition; the turn of a head, the twist of a body are calculated so as to heighten the character of the theme. The painting itself with its fabulous colours (some passages are more robust than others) is an exuberant affirmation of hedonism; it is not gross, however, and the touch, if broad, has great refinement. The delicacy of the treatment may be observed in the way the eye is taken from figure to figure, from the man drinking on the left, via his companions pouring out libations and holding a jug aloft, to the girl overcome by drink. Her pose looks back to some antique prototype and forward to certain paintings by Courbet.

Titian's pre-eminence as a colourist hardly requires emphasis; his prowess as a designer was equally remarkable. This faculty is well to the fore in the paintings done for Alfonso. The "Bacchus and Ariadne" is a remarkable example of subtle contrivance, each portion contributing to the thematic harmony and to the vital equilibrium. Bacchus is the key figure. Wearing a crimson robe, caught by the wind, and turning his body, as if sculpted by a Hellenistic artist, he both embodies the movement, essential to the picture, and helps to carry it forward. His sense of urgency is balanced by Ariadne's pointing ahead, as if to continue her flight. It is a moment of tense excitement; and the emotional content is paralleled by the richness of the colours—a detail like the cheetahs (expressly mentioned by Philostratus) is particularly fine.

In the 1510s and 1520s, when he was engaged on these tasks, which must have proved congenial, Titian was also occupied with other, very different pictures. He was entrusted with a number of large-scale and important religious commissions; these brought him into the front rank of High Renaissance art. There is an astonishing contrast in mood between the triumphant "Assumption of the Virgin" (p. 36) painted for Santa Maria dei Frari, Venice, between 1516-1518 and the polytych

17

altarpiece depicting the Resurrection (p. 33) executed in 1520-1522 for SS. Nazaro e Celso at Brescia. The former, which betrays Raphaelesque influences, is a noble atmospheric composition, almost proto Counter Reformation in spirit. The latter has a more mannerist twist to it; this is especially evident in the figure of St. Stephen which may have been partly derived from the famous Hellenistic or Roman sculpture of the Laocoon, after which Titian made a curious caricature-like woodcut. (A derivation from Michelangelo has also been proposed.) Both pictures, in any case, indicate his under-standing of the problems involved in formulating large reli-gious compositions; and the "Resurrection" once more reveal-ed his sense for drama.

The grandiloquence of Titian's visual language comes over in the celebrated "Madonna of the Pesaro Family" (p. 37) in Santa Maria dei Frari at Venice, which was painted between 1519 and 1526. This constitutes a break with the old conception of representing the Madonna and Child in the centre of the stage; Titian placed them in a raised position to the right; yet they remain the focus of attention. Moreover, instead of the conventional landscape background, columns are introduced; these add that note of ceremonial pomp, which, later, Veronese exploited so happily. There is also the customary love of the intimate detail; one which gives an individuality to the picture; in this case, the vivacious Christ Child who lifts the Virgin's headdress.

Titian's aim was to relate the disparate elements in the composi-tion to each other by means either of chromatic interplay or else by a bold manipulation of the figures in the picture space. Thus in the "Murder of St. Peter Martyr", which was painted between 1525 and 1530 for SS. Giovanni e Paolo at Venice and is now destroyed, the movement of the murderer, the friar in flight and the trees all point the eye in the same direc-

18

(Continued on page 73)

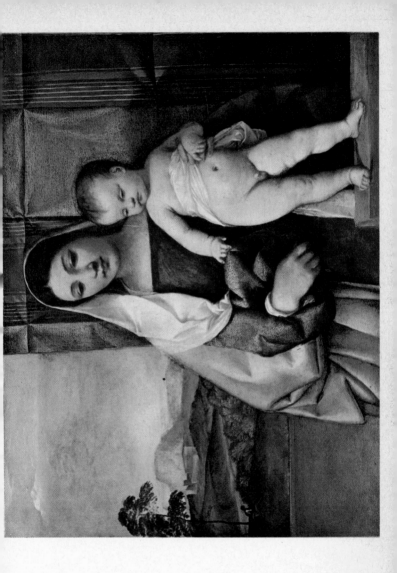

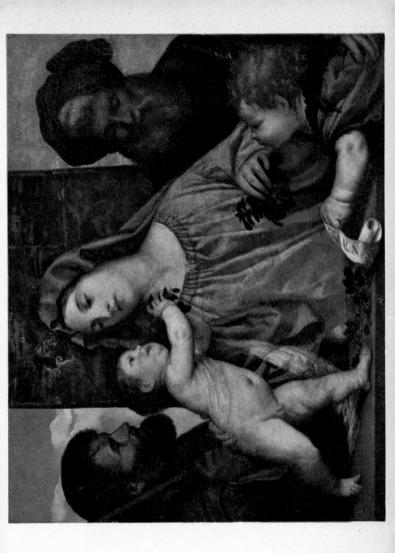

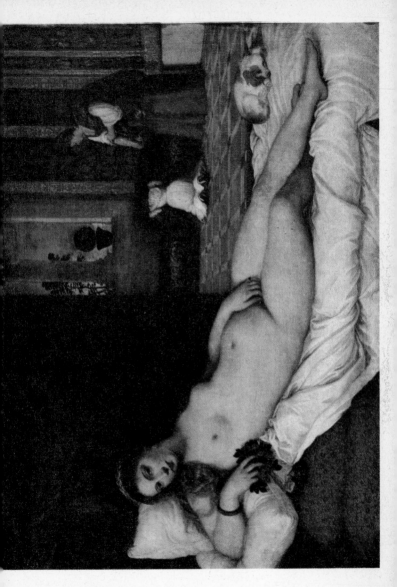

40

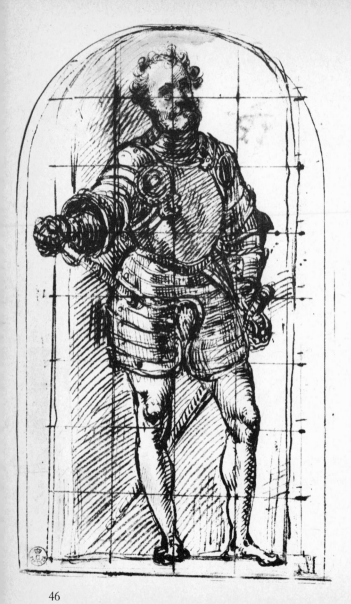

46

50

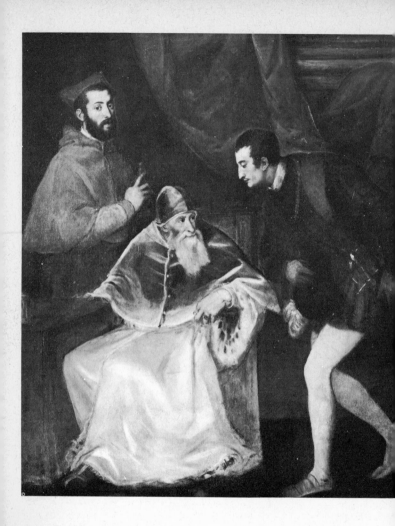

53

58

tion. This provides an illustration, as Wölfflin once observed, of the system of perfection described by L. B. Alberti under which the smallest part could not be changed without marring the beauty of the whole. It is this sense of careful planning and of the relationship between form and colour which distinguishes "The Entombment" (p. 42) of about 1525, in the Louvre.

His skill in presenting dramatic events makes the loss of the "Battle of Cadore" particularly grave. This was completed for the Great Hall of the Ducal Palace in Venice by 1538 and was obviously a picture of major significance; the composition (known from a print and a drawing) bears comparison with Leonardo's "Battle of the Anghiari" and Raphael's "Victory of Constantine".

In these pictures, as in his religious works, Titian showed a remarkable adaptability. One of his most attractive traits was the art of making his religious pictures seem human and intimate. They are given a freedom which brings them close to the spectator, as can be seen in the lovely "Assumption" of the early 1530s in the Cathedral at Verona, and this is the quality which distinguishes his smaller works as well, notably the tender "Madonna with the Rabbit" (p. 41) of 1530, in the Louvre, where the colours are associated into a delicate harmony. Indeed, one well understands that for the writers of the 16th and 17th centuries, Titian stood out as the painter of reality. Thus Dolce declared that in his paintings "Life itself is not more lifelike". Biondo stated that "All that Titian's figures want is a voice; in all else they are nature itself". For Boschini "he was the very mirror of nature, only that the mirror reflects whilst Titian creates".

This love of the human touch is evident in the "Presentation of the Virgin in the Temple" (1534-1538: p. 40) in the Accademia, Venice, which is in line with the tradition of narrative painting associated with Carpaccio. His faculty of observation is striking;

73

the old peasant with her basket of eggs is an essay in realism and seems to anticipate the approach employed by Caravaggio in the 1600s. Then the classical torso, casually placed on the right, forms an exquisite passage of tonal painting. Titian's mastery of positioning allowed him to introduce a variety of different human types into the picture and yet avoid overcrowding, usually the bane of such scenes; and here the assembly does not detract from the small and tender figure of the Virgin mounting the steps—themselves admirably realised cubic blocks. In this majestic picture the statuesque figures award the scene the solemnity of a moment of religious grandeur—it is as if it takes place to the accompaniment of a mighty organ peal.

A marked change occurred in Titian's art in the 1540s. He drew close to the troubled preoccupations of the Central Italian painters. The "Ecce Homo" at Vienna (p. 62), which was painted in 1543 for a Flemish merchant, is couched in the narrative manner of the "Presentation of the Virgin in the Temple" but the difference is striking; where once had been calm, now there was unrest. The detail of the boy on the steps is an indication of this new mood. It is an important document for the development of Titian's mind, as well as of his art, and it is reasonable to suppose that, like many of his contemporaries, he was affected by the religious crisis of the time. His visit to Rome in 1543-46 must have made him aware of the new currents and his first version of the "Martyrdom of St. Lawrence" in the Jesuiti at Venice, with its echoes from Raphael, reveals his contact with the Roman milieu; it is a picture of dramatic light with a touch of despair.

One of the most important pictures dating from the 1540s, which was probably painted shortly before his journey to Rome, was the impressive "Votive Picture of the Vendramin Family" (p. 63) in the National Gallery, London. In this daring and harmonious large-scale work, the observation of the differ-

74

ent types represented is as perceptive as their arrangement is skilful; the individuality of the poses, the gorgeousness of the robes, the contrasts of colour—these contribute to the stateliness of the scene and its sense of awe. The centre of attention is focussed on the candlestick on the altar (p. 54)—a wonderful passage of still-life painting, touched in with bold, almost quivering colours. In another respect, the painting is appealing; namely in the portraits of the various members of the family. Already in the "Madonna of the Pesaro Family" (p. 37), Titian had distinguished himself by the tenderness of the portraits—those renderings of Venetian patricians which suggest a link with the patient assessment of the donors so typical of early Flemish art. He had in such portraits the knack of making contrasts: the youth, for instance, with his almost Raphaelesque smoothness of features who stares out of the picture, as if to set off the devotion of his elders, and a similar passage is found in "The Vendramin Family".

Titian was a great portrait painter and in Ricketts' opinion even the greatest of them all. His early portraits, like the "Portrait of a Man" in the National Gallery (p. 20) or the "Man with a Glove" (p. 39) in the Louvre, are tender and refined; the latter has a marvellous detail of still-life—the hand with the glove, which looks like a foretaste of Van Dyck. He possessed the correct blend of deference and distance required to make him the chosen portrait painter of the upper ranks of international society. He virtually became the recorder of the main political figures of his era when he was staying at the Imperial Court of Augsburg in 1548-1549 and 1550-1551. In fact our impressions of Francis I, Philip II, Charles V, the Empress Isabella (p. 57) and the Dukes of Mantua are largely culled from his portraits, even if, as sometimes happened, his renderings were based on another artist's depiction of the same sitter. How extraordinarily engaging is the elegant, foppish

75

figure of Federigo Gonzaga in the Prado, Madrid (p. 38), one of whose hands caresses a dog; his blue and white cuffs are as delicately treated as in a pastel by Perronneau. Titian could fill a canvas so that the personality seems to burst out of the frame; this is certainly the impression made by his virile "Portrait of Aretino" in the Palazzo Pitti, Florence. And he could ring the changes on a variety of moods; he catches a note of restless anxiety in the "Portrait of Ippolito Riminaldi" in the Palazzo Pitti, Florence, of tenderness in the "Man with a Cross" in the Prado, Madrid. The "Portrait of Pope Paul III with his Nephews" (p. 52) in the Museo Nazionale, Naples, is one of the frankest portraits of the 16th century in which the foxy craftiness of the Pope is balanced by the servile cringing of the "Nephews".

There must be some truth in Georg Gronau's contention that its unfinished state is due to the annoyance it caused. He was one of the first men to securely establish the sitter's stance in a full-length portrait, as may be seen in the drawing (p. 46) in the Uffizi, Florence, for the portrait of the Duke of Urbino, the so-called "Duke of Atri", at Kassel (p. 53) or in the "Philip II" in the Prado. This is surely one reason for his appeal to Veláz-quez. His sensitive understanding of psychology may be observed in the famous, if rather damaged, portrait of "Charles V on Horseback" (p. 47) in the Prado; this is a haunting, almost symbolical image; the Emperor looks like the last knight in Christendom, a sort of majestic Don Quixote, poised for his entry into the new and modern world.

Titian's art constitutes a deep homage to woman. In his early years he had celebrated the charms of the Giorgionesque beauty and of the courtesan. His single studies of such figures are amongst the most noble and glorious creations of the Italian genius, palpable and alluring. In the 1530s, doubtless in response to the demands of his patrons, he created what was virtually a new genre—the domestic nude. "The Venus of

76

Self-portrait
About 1565; oil on canvas; 34×25¾ in.;
Prado, Madrid

Urbino (p. 35) in the Uffizi, Florence, is perhaps the most seductive. She has nothing aloof about her; she is a person. This must be one of the first female nudes painted with a full recognition of the subject's sexual appeal, and the difference between her and the women in the earlier pictures is subtle but distinctive; she may be considered as the ancestress of the women painted by Velázquez, Goya, Delacroix, Corot and Manet. Titian so heightens our apprehension of life that certain moods and experiences almost invariably bring to mind pictures of this sort.

It is significant that Moravia should have introduced the early version of the "Danaë" at Naples into one of his novels—and at a moment of ecstasy. It is this nude which illustrates the changes which occurred in Titian's art during the 1540s. The picture was apparently painted in Rome, in the Belvedere, and an echo of the classical background may be seen in the cupid, which is of Praxitelean type, while Danaë herself is possibly based on one of Michelangelo's river gods. The effects of the alteration in his style which now intervened are more apparent in the golden "Danaë" (p. 67) in the Prado, Madrid; her body is relaxed with warm sensual anticipation, so that we are left in no doubt that, for her, existence is centred on the bed. A sculptural quality is still retained but the artist's main aim was the blending of colours into a consistent harmony—one which replaced any idea of representing form by linear means.

Titian's final phase is complex and profound. He was to die in 1576, a victim of the plague. During the last twenty-five years of his life, he achieved, progressively, a new and extraordinary style, one which is all the more surprising in view of his great age.

So considerable is the difference between the pictures of the 1540s and those painted in the following decade that it is tempting to fuse the work of this last part of his life into one period and thus to overlook that it continued over nearly a quarter of a century. Moreover, the differences that occur between one sort of painting and another are extremely relevant. In general, for instance, one might be inclined to maintain that many of the religious pictures painted from 1550 onwards are pessimistic in tone; they take the tragic rather than the happy theme. Yet in a work like "La Gloria" in the Prado, Madrid (p. 59), which was started in 1551, confidence in the Almighty is explicit. This is a particularly sonorous picture in which the figures are woven into a design which ascends upwards with supreme assurance while the colours, reds, blues, browns, greens, create a mood of peace.

The "Danaë" (p. 67) at Madrid reveals the extent to which Titian had become a painter of remembrance as well as of discovery. Old men muse, and in a number of his later pictures, Titian seems to do the same. This selective treatment of experiences lies behind the majestic series of "poesies" which he painted in the 1550s and 1560s for Philip II of Spain. These mythological pictures designed as decorations for the walls of the Royal Palace at Madrid stand in the history of European art as great theatrical compositions—operatic in their volume, radical in the gradated explosiveness of colour. In them, as in the pictures painted for the Estes, Titian explored the world of antique mythology, and in his interpretation the stories are pristine and exciting. One feels that never before and never since have the legends of "Perseus and Andromeda" (Wallace Collection, London: p. 60), "The Rape of Europa" (Isabella Stewart Gardner Museum, Boston; p. 61) or the "Death of Actaeon" (Earl of Harewood, Yorkshire; p. 45) been treated with such nobility and invention.

Just as he turned his sitters (whether they deserved this status or not) into aristocrats, so he turned such subjects into the fitting decoration for a palace. They are pictures which bring us up to their level; make us, as it were, walk on spring-heeled boots. Any idea of a conventional perspective is abandoned; the artist created a tapestry-like effect in which the blurred and blended colours in the background permit a romantic illusionism. This is painting which translates the spectator into a world which exists in its own right—in terms of colour. The danger that too uniform a surface might have deadened the picture was overcome by the vivacity of the brush strokes. The surface in fact is worked up and over—one layer harmonizing with the other so that when all was ready, the introduction of areas of accented colour gave life to the whole picture. The colours feed each other, and draw their final, enduring splendour from the blues and greens which vivify the darker tones. The consequence of this approach was that no single portion was separated from its neighbour: they were unified. The start of a process in which landscape, for instance, was no longer placed as a background to the figures and could be removed from them may be seen in "The Pardo Venus" in the Louvre, and its fulfilment came in the "Death of Actaeon" —that so magical and mysterious picture which throbs with chromatic vitality. The details reproduced on pages 44 and 45 point the contrast.

Not all the late secular pictures treated the subjects in so colourful a manner. In certain works, like the "Lucretia and Tarquin" (p. 51) in the Fitzwilliam Museum, Cambridge, this dynamic pictorial treatment was used to achieve a stark vision —a moment of brutality in this case, which recalls the early "Jealous Husband" (p. 24) and which anticipates Caravaggesque realism. It was a vision verging on the horrific, and one of his last pictures, the astonishing "Flaying of Marsyas" (Archiepiscopal Palace, Kremsier: p. 58) has a touch of hallucination about it; this, one feels, is a dream which has to be exorcised.

Study of a man
About 1550-55; black and white chalks on grey paper;
10¼ × 7⅜ in.; private collection, London

To turn back and look at the early pictures is to realise the extent of the changes which had taken place in Titian's art, as in Venetian painting in general. When Titian started, the ideals of the Quattrocento, devout, secure and contained, were predominant; he was to live almost to the end of a century in which everything was increasingly questioned. He did not fail to keep abreast of such currents. The development of his final style, moreover, owed much to his failing eyesight and trembling hand; such factors forced him to generalise rather than particularise. Thus he was compelled to adopt a way of painting in which the distinction between the sketch and the finished picture was broken down. Fortunately, Palma Giovane has left a description of his technique at this stage which, though well known, deserves to be quoted—and for modernists, the attention Titian so evidently gave to "marks" on the canvas will be especially fascinating:

"Titian began his pictures with a mass of colour which served as a bed or foundation for what he wished to express. I myself have seen such vigorously applied under-painting in pure red ochre, which was meant to give the half-tone, or in white lead. With the same brush, which he dipped in red, black or yellow, he created the plastic effect of the light portions. With four strokes he was capable of indicating a magnificent figure. Sketches of this kind were of the greatest interest to connoisseurs, because they showed the way to true painting. After he had thus applied this important foundation, he turned the pictures to the wall and left them, without looking at them, sometimes for months. When he afterwards returned to them, he scanned them with a concentration as severe as if they had been his mortal enemies, in order to find faults in them; and if he found something which was not in accord with his intentions, he went to work like a surgeon who ruthlessly removes a tumour, or sets an arm, or brings a displaced foot into the correct position. Thus, by repeated revision, he brought the skeleton of his figures to the highest degree of perfection and, while one picture was drying, he turned to another. This quintessence of a composition he then covered with many layers of living flesh, until the figure seemed to lack only breadth. He never painted a figure *alla prima*,* and was wont to say that he who improvises can never fashion a perfect line of poetry. He gave the last touch to his pictures by adjusting with his fingers the transitions from the highest lights to the half-tones or he would apply a spot of black in one corner or heighten with a dab of red, like a drop of blood, the liveliness of the surface; and thus he gradually brought his figures to completion. In the last stages of the work, he painted more with his fingers than with the brush . . ."

The effects of this technique may be clearly seen in his late religious pictures—the fabulous "St. Margaret" (p. 70) in the Prado, with the burning city in the background and the impressionistic rocks, the "St. Sebastian" (p. 50) in the Hermitage and the resigned "Christ Crowned with Thorns" (p. 64) at Munich. It is almost with a gasp that one realises that this is the painter of the "Sacred and Profane Love", of the "Assumption" in the Frari, of "La Bella". No note of pleasure now occurs; no sense of radiance; no passion for sunlit fields. Titian has become the painter of a nocturnal world in which the sun has sunk, in which flares and torches are the accompaniments to the inevitability of death. But the overwhelming sense of finality which now intervenes does not hamper his genius, and in the "Christ in the Garden of Gethsemane" in the Prado, a picture which has suffered greatly and defies reproduction, the scene is rendered by suggestion—so vital is this that we seem to hear the trudge of the soldiers as they close in on Christ. We are led

*alla prima: application of paint by an artist to his final conception without any previous planning in the form of a drawing or sketch.

into the doom-laden atmosphere of Caravaggio. And in the "Pieta" (p. 72) in the Accademia at Venice, which the old painter left unfinished at his death and which Palma Giovane completed, the very lions seem to weep. It is a stark and demanding attack upon our pity.

Two Kneeling Boys in a Landscape
About 1510; pen drawing; 9¼ × 8⅜ in.;
Albertina, Vienna

84

LIST OF ILLUSTRATIONS

29 SACRED AND PROFANE LOVE
About 1515; oil on canvas; 46¾ × 111 in.;
Galleria Borghese, Rome

30 BACCHANAL (The Andrians)
About 1518-19; signed: Ticianus f.; oil on canvas;
69 × 76 in.;
Prado, Madrid

31 BACCHUS AND ARIADNE
About 1523; signed: Ticianus f.; oil on canvas; 69 × 75 in.;
National Gallery, London

32 ST. SEBASTIAN
About 1522; drawing; 7¼ × 4¾ in.;
Staedelsches Kunstinstitut, Frankfurt-am-Main

33 ST. SEBASTIAN
Signed and dated 1522; oil on panel; 66 × 25 in.; part of the
altarpiece of the Resurrection, SS. Nazaro e Celso, Brescia

34 THE FEAST OF VENUS
About 1516-18; oil on canvas; 68 × 68¾ in.;
Prado, Madrid

35 THE VENUS OF URBINO
Around 1538; oil on canvas; 47¼ × 65 in.;
Uffizi, Florence

36 THE ASSUMPTION OF THE VIRGIN
1516-18; signed: Ticianus; oil on canvas; 272 × 142 in.;
Santa Maria dei Frari, Venice

37 MADONNA OF THE PESARO FAMILY
1519-26; on canvas; 191 × 106½ in.;
Santa Maria dei Frari, Venice

38 FEDERIGO II GONZAGA, DUKE OF MANTUA
About 1525; signed: Ticianus F.; oil on wood; 49¼ × 39¼ in.;
Prado, Madrid

39 MAN WITH A GLOVE
   About 1520-27; oil on canvas; 39½×35 in.;
   Louvre, Paris

40 PRESENTATION OF THE VIRGIN (detail: old woman in the
   foreground)
   1534-38; oil on canvas; Accademia, Venice

41 MADONNA WITH THE RABBIT
   About 1530; oil on canvas; 27¾ × 33 in; Louvre, Paris

42 THE ENTOMBMENT
   About 1525; oil on canvas; 58¾×86¾ in.; Louvre, Paris

43 ST. JEROME IN A LANDSCAPE
   About 1535; oil on canvas; 31½×40½ in.; Louvre, Paris

44 THE PARDO VENUS (detail of landscape)
   About 1540; oil on canvas; Louvre, Paris

45 DIANA AND ACTAEON, also called DEATH OF ACTAEON (detail
   of landscape)
   About 1559; oil on canvas; Earl of Harewood collection,
   on loan to the National Gallery, London

46 FRANCESCO MARIA DELLA ROVERE, DUKE OF URBINO
   About 1536; drawing; 9½×5⅞ in.; Uffizi, Florence

47 CHARLES V ON HORSEBACK
   1548; oil on canvas; 131×110½ in.; Prado, Madrid

48 DIANA AND ACTAEON
   1559, oil on canvas; 75 × 81¾ in.; The Earl of Ellesmere
   collection, on loan to the National Gallery of Scotland,
   Edinburgh

49 CHILD WITH DOGS
   About 1565; oil on canvas; 50½×71 in.;
   Van Beuningen-Boymans Museum, Rotterdam